GENDER HEROES

OF RELATED INTEREST

SYLVIA AND MARSHA START A REVOLUTION!
The Story of the Trans Women of Color
Who Made LGBTQ+ History
Joy Ellison | Illustrated by Teshika Silver
ISBN 978 1 78775 530 7
EISBN 978 1 78775 531 4

THE PRONOUN BOOK
She, He, They, and Me!
Cassandra Jules Corrigan | Illustrated by Jem Milton
ISBN 978 1 78775 957 2
EISBN 978 1 78775 958 9

THE BIG BOOK OF PRIDE FLAGS
Illustrated by Jem Milton
ISBN 978 1 83997 258 4
EISBN 978 1 83997 259 1

LGBTQIA+ PRIDE STICKER BOOK
Illustrated by Ollie Mann
ISBN 978 1 83997 246 1
EISBN 978 1 83997 259 1

GENDER HEROES

25 Amazing Transgender, Non-Binary and Genderqueer
Trailblazers from **Past** and **Present**!

ILLUSTRATED BY FILIPA NAMORADO

Jessica Kingsley Publishers
London and Philadelphia

First published in Great Britain in 2023 by Jessica Kingsley Publishers
An imprint of Hodder & Stoughton Ltd
An Hachette Company

1

Copyright © Jessica Kingsley Publishers 2023
Illustration Copyright © Filipa Namorado 2023

A CIP catalogue record for this title is available from the British Library
and the Library of Congress

ISBN 978 1 83997 325 3
eISBN 978 1 83997 326 0

Printed and bound in China by Leo Paper Products Ltd

Jessica Kingsley Publishers' policy is to use papers that are natural,
renewable and recyclable products and made from wood grown
in sustainable forests. The logging and manufacturing processes
are expected to conform to the environmental regulations
of the country of origin.

Jessica Kingsley Publishers
Carmelite House
50 Victoria Embankment
London EC4Y 0DZ

www.jkp.com

INTRODUCTION

There have been many amazing cisgender men and women throughout history who have changed the world. But what about all the incredible transgender, non-binary and gender non-conforming people who have equally transformed our lives?

This book introduces you to 25 incredible gender pioneers whose remarkable bravery, resilience and achievements—across art, sport, fashion, music, politics, civil rights and the media—have blazed a trail for other trans people.

These are people who have had to fight to be themselves, and in doing so, have enabled others to be true to who they are. They have shown the world there is no right or wrong way to express your gender. Whoever you are and whatever your gender, you are free to express your identity however you want.

Every person in this book is a reminder to you that not all heroes wear capes—they dress and express themselves and live their lives however they choose.

We are each of us, in our own unique way, a gender hero and every one of us has the power to change the world!

MARSHA P. JOHNSON

Marsha P. Johnson was a Black transgender woman who revolutionized LGBTQIA+ rights.

Marsha was an activist, drag queen and performer and one of the central figures in the Stonewall Uprising. This was a movement that began after a group of LGBTQIA+ individuals stood up for themselves against a police raid at New York City's Stonewall Inn in 1969. Along with her friends, Sylvia Rivera and Stormé DeLarverie, Marsha helped start the uprising, sparking a resistance movement around the world that transformed LGBTQIA+ rights. Marsha dedicated her life to helping others and founded an organization to support gay and trans youth who were homeless.

In 2020, in honor of Marsha's empowering bravery and courage, the City of New York renamed the East River State Park in Brooklyn the Marsha P. Johnson State Park, and activists erected a statue of Marsha in Christopher Park in 2021. Marsha's statue was one of the world's first monuments in honor of a transgender person.

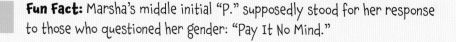 **Fun Fact:** Marsha's middle initial "P." supposedly stood for her response to those who questioned her gender: "Pay It No Mind."

ELLIOT PAGE

Elliot Page is a trans man and one of the most talented actors of his generation.

Elliot received critical acclaim for playing the role of Juno in the film of the same name. For his performance, Elliot was nominated for multiple awards including an Academy Award and a Golden Globe. Elliot is also famous for playing the role of Vanya—who transitions in season 3 to become Viktor—in the Netflix series *The Umbrella Academy*, for which he was nominated for two Primetime Emmy Awards.

Elliot is a fierce advocate for trans people, especially trans youth, and he has become one of the most vocal transgender activists and best-known transmasculine people in the world.

 Fun Fact: Elliot was the first openly transgender man to appear on the cover of *TIME* magazine.

CHARLIE CRAGGS

Charlie Craggs is fighting transphobia and prejudice one fabulous manicure at a time.

Realizing there wasn't enough support for young trans women, Charlie launched Nail Transphobia—a campaign where she provided free manicures to people, allowing them to meet and speak with a trans person and learn about their experiences, while receiving glamorously painted nails. Nail Transphobia sought to combat transphobia and negative stereotypes about trans people by educating people about the lived realities of being a trans person today.

Through her activism, Charlie has become one of the most influential and empowering trans people in the UK. In 2017, she published *To My Trans Sisters*—a collection of letters written by trailblazing trans women, addressed to other trans women—which has since become a touchstone for trans women everywhere.

 Fun Fact: Charlie was instrumental in successfully getting the transgender flag emoji included by Unicode after a successful campaign.

SARAH MCBRIDE

Sarah McBride is the first openly transgender state senator in the United States of America.

In November 2020, Sarah won a seat in the Delaware Senate and was instrumental in lobbying to pass a law in the state of Delaware that prohibited discrimination based on gender identity. In 2016, she spoke at the Democratic National Convention, making her the first openly transgender person to address a major party convention in the history of America.

Sarah's victory shows all of us that we can achieve whatever we dream. On winning her election she said: "I hope tonight shows an LGBTQ kid that our democracy is big enough for them, too."

 Fun Fact: Sarah is the highest-ranking transgender elected official in American history.

SYLVIA RIVERA

Throughout her life, Sylvia Rivera campaigned tirelessly for equal rights for trans people.

Sylvia was a Latinx transgender activist who is said to have helped start the Stonewall Uprising alongside her closest friend, Marsha P. Johnson. Following the riots, Sylvia was an active member of the Gay Liberation Front and fought for the inclusion of trans people in the gay rights movement. With Marsha P. Johnson, Sylvia helped form an organization to support gay and trans youth who were homeless.

Sylvia's legacy lives on today through the Sylvia Rivera Law Project, which "works to guarantee that all people are free to self-determine their gender identity and expression, regardless of income or race."

 Fun Fact: Sylvia was once arrested after climbing the walls of City Hall in a dress and high heels to crash a meeting on a gay rights bill.

CHELLA MAN

Chella Man is a celebrated Deaf, trans, Jewish and Chinese artist, actor and model.

Chella Man made history as the first Deaf and transmasculine model to be signed by a modeling agency, as well as the first transmasculine actor to be cast in a DC superhero series, playing Jericho in *Titans*. He published his first book, *Continuum*, with Penguin, and he has written for the pioneering queer publication *Them*.

Through his acting, art and writing, Chella Man pushes the boundaries of what it means to be equal and inclusive in today's world and he has become a hugely popular role model for people from marginalized communities.

Fun Fact: Chella Man rose to fame via his YouTube channel, which has over 250,000 subscribers!

OWL AND FOX FISHER

Owl and Fox Fisher are a leading non-binary couple whose activism, writing and filmmaking has revolutionized trans representation in the media.

Owl and Fox co-founded My Genderation—a film project that celebrates trans lives and experiences—and they have created over 100 short films, which have won numerous awards and featured at film festivals around the world. Through their work with All About Trans—an organization that seeks to improve trans representation in the media—their writing for leading news publications, and their various TEDx Talks and media appearances, Owl and Fox have become two of the most powerful and forward-thinking voices in the trans community.

 Fun Fact: Fox co-founded Trans Pride Brighton—the first trans pride event outside of America—and Owl, who is Icelandic, ran for parliament in Iceland in 2018 and 2019.

JAZZ JENNINGS

Jazz Jennings has transformed the representation and awareness of trans youth by always being true to herself.

At six years old, Jazz appeared on television to speak about being transgender and the interview changed her life forever. In the years after the interview, she launched her popular reality TV show *I Am Jazz*, led the New York City Pride parade as its youngest grand marshal, co-wrote a children's book and won a GLAAD Media Award. With her parents she also founded Transkids Purple Rainbow Foundation to support other transgender youth.

A fierce LGBTQIA+ activist, Jazz has been an inspiration to young trans kids everywhere and has shown the power in allowing trans kids to speak for themselves.

 Fun Fact: Jazz is one of the youngest people to be publicly documented as trans.

MAUREE TURNER

Mauree Turner is the first openly non-binary state legislator in the history of the United States of America.

When Mauree was elected State Representative for Oklahoma's 88th House District, they also became Oklahoma's first Muslim lawmaker. Mauree has dedicated their life to fighting for immigration rights, racial justice and criminal justice.

Mauree is blazing a trail for non-binary people and their courage is an inspiration to anyone who wants to change the world.

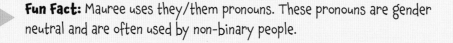 **Fun Fact:** Mauree uses they/them pronouns. These pronouns are gender neutral and are often used by non-binary people.

FREDDY MCCONNELL

Freddy McConnell is the first trans man in the UK to conceive and give birth to his own child.

In 2016, Freddy documented his journey to fatherhood as a trans man in the widely acclaimed film *Seahorse: The Dad Who Gave Birth*.

Although Freddy lost a legal battle to be listed as the father of his child, his story and activism have helped transform society's understanding of what it means to be a father, as well as raising awareness of queer birth and families.

 Fun Fact: The film *Seahorse* is named after the fact that male seahorses are the only males in the animal kingdom who carry and give birth to their offspring.

LAVERNE COX

Laverne Cox is one of the most famous and successful Black transgender women working in film and television today.

Laverne's road to stardom began with the ground-breaking role of Sophia Burset in the acclaimed series *Orange Is the New Black*. The role led to Laverne being the first trans woman to be nominated for a Primetime Emmy Award for acting. In 2020, she produced the documentary *Disclosure*, which examined the representation of transgender people in film and television. It was named one of the 100 best documentaries of all time by *Vogue*.

Laverne is a trailblazer for trans people everywhere, who seeks to empower others to move beyond gender expectations and to live authentically.

 Fun Fact: Laverne was the first openly transgender person to appear on the cover of *TIME* magazine.

ALOK VAID-MENON

Alok Vaid-Menon is an internationally acclaimed writer, performer and speaker who uses their work to break the gender binary.

As a gender non-conforming, transfeminine person of color, Alok's art and performances explore trauma, race, gender and belonging and they have performed at 600 venues in 40 countries around the world. They have also published a number of books including *Beyond the Gender Binary* and designed three gender-neutral fashion collections.

Alok's creative work is an inspiration to others to challenge the status quo, and gives people permission to express themselves however they want.

 Fun Fact: Alok is the creator of #DeGenderFashion—a movement that seeks to make the fashion industry more inclusive.

CHRIS MOSIER

Chris Mosier is a ground-breaking transgender athlete and sportsperson.

Chris was the first openly transgender man to represent the United States in an Olympic trial event and was the catalyst for the International Olympic Committee to change its guidelines on participation for transgender athletes.

Chris is a six-time member of Team USA, the first transgender athlete sponsored by Nike, he was chosen as Outsports Person of the Year in 2016 and was the first openly transgender man to be inducted into the National Gay and Lesbian Sports Hall of Fame.

 Fun Fact: Chris is the founder of transathlete.com, a resource for students, athletes and coaches to help find information about trans inclusion in athletics.

MICHAELA JAÉ RODRIGUEZ

Michaela Jaé Rodriguez is a pioneering Black Latinx actress.

In 2017, Michaela was cast as a lead role in the television series *Pose*, making her part of the largest cast of transgender actors to star as regulars in a scripted series, revolutionizing trans representation on TV.

For her ground-breaking performance as Blanca Evangelista, Michaela became the first openly transgender woman to earn an Emmy Award acting nomination. In 2021, she was nominated for Outstanding Lead Actress in a Drama Series and in 2022 she made history as the first transgender woman to win the Golden Globe Award for Best Actress—Television Series Drama.

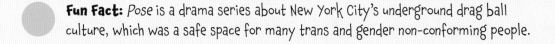 **Fun Fact:** *Pose* is a drama series about New York City's underground drag ball culture, which was a safe space for many trans and gender non-conforming people.

AARON ROSE PHILIP

Aaron Rose Philip made fashion history as the first Black, transgender and physically disabled person to be signed by a major modeling agency.

Aaron has cerebral palsy and actively campaigns to increase representation of trans women of color and disabled people in the fashion world. She has been photographed for *Vogue* and *British Vogue* and appeared in adverts for Nike.

Aaron's ambition and fearlessness are a powerful reminder that if you have faith in yourself, you can always reach your goals.

 Fun Fact: Aaron was the first model to use a wheelchair on the runway for a leading luxury fashion brand.

REBEKAH BRUESEHOFF

Rebekah Bruesehoff is a transgender teen activist who is fighting to make the world a better place for transgender kids everywhere.

When she was 10 years old, Rebekah spoke at a rally after the Trump administration had tried to take away certain rights for transgender students. After a picture of Rebekah holding a sign that read "I'm the scary transgender person the media warned you about" went viral, she decided to use her new platform to make sure every transgender child is heard.

Rebekah continues to spread her message of hope for transgender youth through her advocacy work and by showing that transgender kids are just like other kids.

 Fun Fact: Rebekah is officially a Marvel superhero after being chosen to be a part of Marvel's Hero Project.

CHARLIE MARTIN

Charlie Martin is the most successful transgender racing car driver in the world.

Charlie is on a mission to be one of the fastest women in Europe. After competing in the Michelin Le Mans Cup in 2019, she is now preparing to become the first openly trans woman to compete in the prestigious 24 Hours of Le Mans—the world's oldest endurance racing event. Often driving at speeds of up to 140 mph, Charlie's bravery and self-belief have helped her to overcome the impossible.

Charlie has fought adversity throughout her life, and in a sport dominated by men, she is championing inclusivity and paving the way for other trans speedsters to take to the track.

 Fun Fact: Charlie was selected as the first Sports Ambassador for leading LGBTQIA+ charity Stonewall.

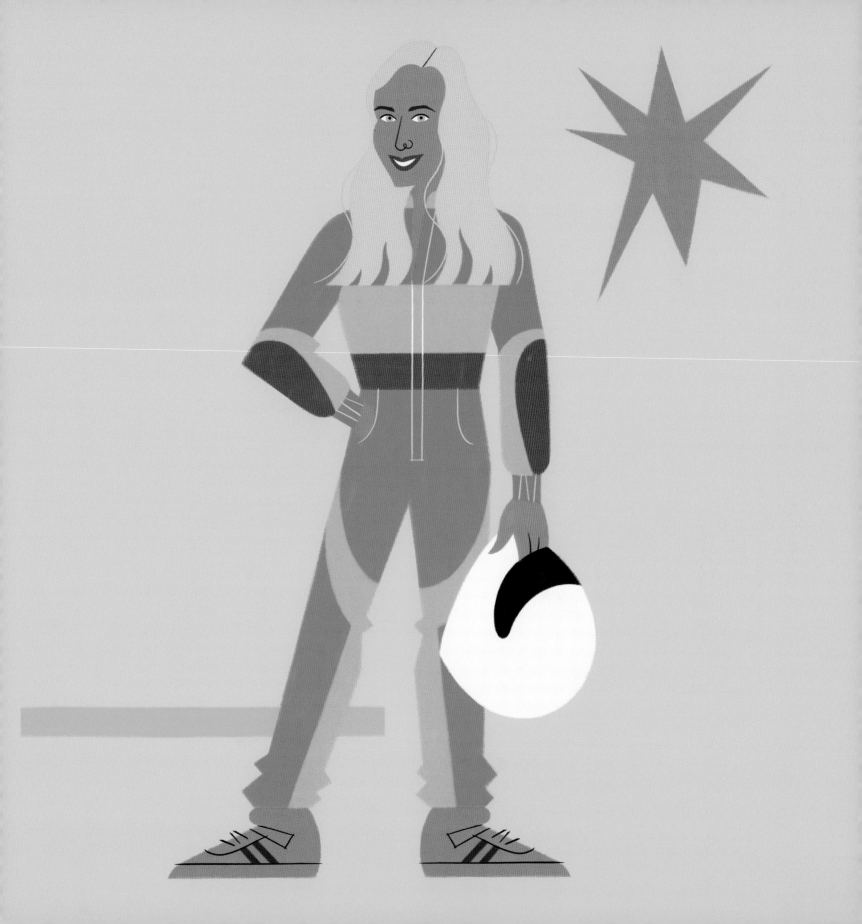

TYLER FORD

Tyler Ford is a visionary trans advocate who is shaping the future of LGBTQIA+ culture.

Tyler is the founder of *Them*—a pioneering online queer platform that has influenced and empowered LGBTQIA+ people worldwide. Their writing and media work highlights their experiences as a queer, transgender person of color and they use their platform to shed light on oppression in everyday life.

Tyler's work has equipped LGBTQIA+ people to express themselves with confidence and is an inspiration to always be yourself and not how others want you to be.

 Fun Fact: Tyler was the first trans contestant on the *Glee* spin-off *The Glee Project*.

MUNROE BERGDORF

Munroe Bergdorf is a world-famous model and activist and the first openly trans model for L'Oréal.

As a mixed-race trans woman, Munroe has used her platform to amplify the voices of marginalized people and in 2018 she released her ground-breaking documentary *What Makes a Woman?* She has received numerous accolades including Changemaker of the Year at the Cosmopolitan Influencer Awards, and the GAY TIMES Honour for British Community Trailblazer.

Throughout her career, Munroe has faced adversity and prejudice, but she has always come back stronger. She is an inspiration to others to stand up for what is right and call out acts of injustice against others.

 Fun Fact: Munroe was the first openly transgender person to appear on the front cover of *Cosmopolitan UK.*

PIDGEON PAGONIS

Pidgeon Pagonis is a non-binary intersex person who is fighting to end intersex surgery on children.

Pigeon is co-founder of the Intersex Justice Project and their #EndIntersexSurgery campaign was successful in getting a hospital in America to halt intersex surgeries. Pidgeon has appeared on the cover of *National Geographic* and was honored as an LGBT Champion of Change in 2015 by Barack Obama.

Pidgeon grew up believing there was no one else like them, but there are about as many intersex people in the world as there are people with red hair! Pidgeon's story is a reminder to all children that you are not alone.

 Fun Fact: Intersex people are born with sex characteristics that do not fit conventional binary notions of male or female bodies.

MISS MAJOR GRIFFIN-GRACY

For over 50 years, Miss Major has dedicated her life to fighting for transgender rights.

As a trans woman of color, Miss Major has fought fiercely to protect other trans women of color. She was the Executive Director of the Transgender Gender-Variant and Intersex Justice Project that works to protect trans people in prisons. She now runs the House of GG, which is a safe haven for trans people in Arkansas.

Now in her eighties, Miss Major's light continues to burn bright and she is a symbol of the modern trans movement.

 Fun Fact: Miss Major was present at the infamous Stonewall Riots in 1969!

KIM PETRAS

Kim Petras is an international LGBTQIA+ pop superstar.

After releasing her debut single, I Don't Want It At All, in 2017 Kim has released numerous pop anthems that have gone viral and resulted in chart success. Born in Germany, she became an icon for young trans people after discussing her gender identity when she was interviewed on national television at age 14.

With her infectious, upbeat songs that are streamed by millions of listeners, Kim has been dubbed by many as the new "princess of pop."

 Fun Fact: Kim was the first openly transgender performer at the MTV Video Music Awards and singer at Macy's Thanksgiving Day Parade.

TRAVIS ALABANZA

Travis Alabanza is an award-winning writer and performer who has been labeled the "future of theater."

After they had a burger thrown at them when walking over a bridge in London, Travis wrote their celebrated play *Burgerz*, which toured internationally to sold-out performances. Their next play, *Overflow*, explored trans safety and was set in a public toilet. They have featured on the Forbes 30 Under 30 List, performed in prestigious venues and given talks around the world on gender, trans identity and race.

Through their performances and poetry, Travis champions choice and autonomy and shows other trans people that the world is full of beautiful possibilities.

 Fun Fact: Travis was the youngest recipient of the Artist-in-Residency program at Tate Galleries.

GAVIN GRIMM

Gavin Grimm won a huge battle for trans rights when he took his high school to court.

Whilst he was still a sophomore student, Gavin sued his school board after being unable to use the men's restrooms after they introduced regulations following complaints from parents. Gavin's case went to District Court and in 2019 it was ruled that the school's bathroom policy had violated the Constitution's Equal Protection Clause as well as Title IX of the Education Amendments of 1972.

Gavin's victory was a beacon of hope for trans students across the United States of America and proof that you are never too young to fight for change.

Fun Fact: Title IX states that no person in the United States shall, based on sex, be excluded from participation in, be denied the benefits of or be subjected to discrimination in any education program.

GLOSSARY

Assigned sex: The sex (male or female) assigned to a child at birth. This is usually based on a child's external anatomy.

Cisgender: A person whose gender identity matches the sex they were assigned at birth.

Gender expression: The way a person expresses their gender identity typically through clothes, style and mannerisms.

Gender identity: A person's internal sense of their own gender, e.g., being male, female, neither of these or both.

Gender non-conforming: A person whose gender identity and gender expression do not match female and male norms.

Genderqueer: An umbrella term for people who identify as neither male nor female, as both or as somewhere in between.

Intersex: A person whose sex characteristics or body do not fit typical definitions of female or male.

LGBTQIA+: An acronym that represents a range of gender identities and sexualities—lesbian, gay, bisexual, transgender, queer, intersex and asexual. The "+" is for those identities not covered by the seven initial letters.

Non-binary: A person whose gender is not exclusively female or male.

Transgender: A person whose gender identity does not match the sex they were assigned at birth.

NOTES